CHRISTMAS
For
DADGAD Guitar

This Book Copyright 2014 By Case Studio Productions

Tea, South Dakota

CHRISTMAS
For
DADGAD Guitar

All Through The Night

Angels We Have Heard On High

Away In A Manger

Deck The Halls

First Noel

Joy To The World

Lullaby

Silent Night

This Book Copyright 2014 By Case Studio Productions

Tea, South Dakota

All Through The Night

DADGAD

Welsh Folksong

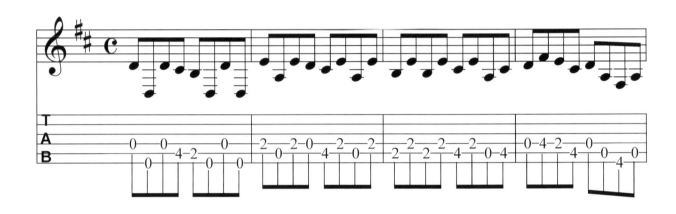

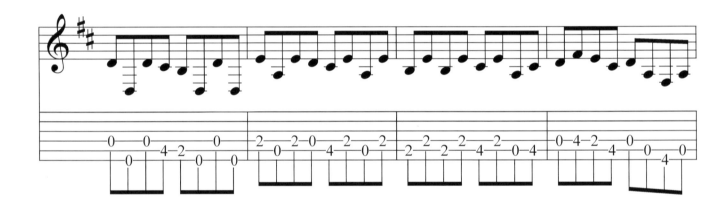

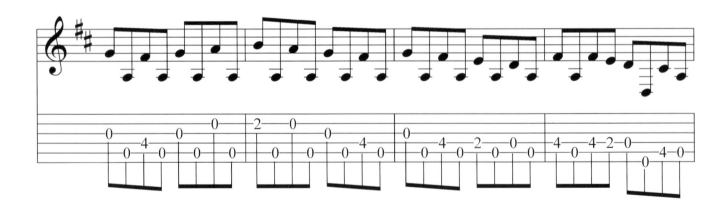

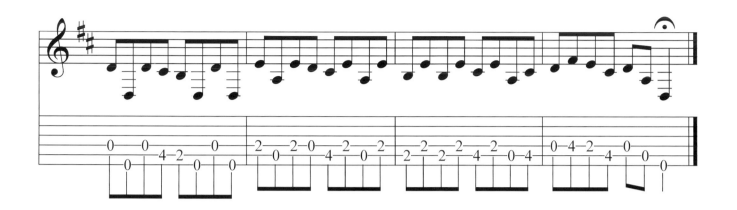

Angels We Have Heard On High

DADGAD

French Carol

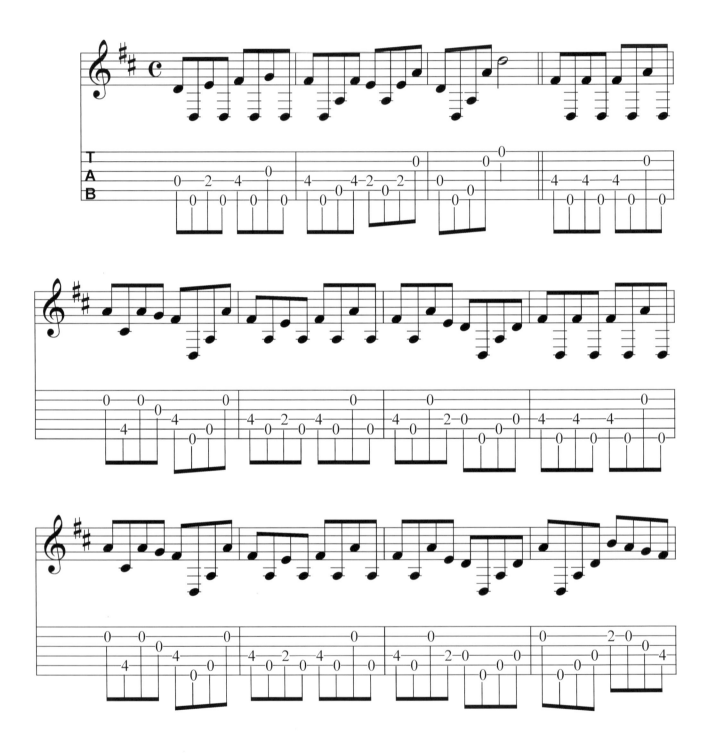

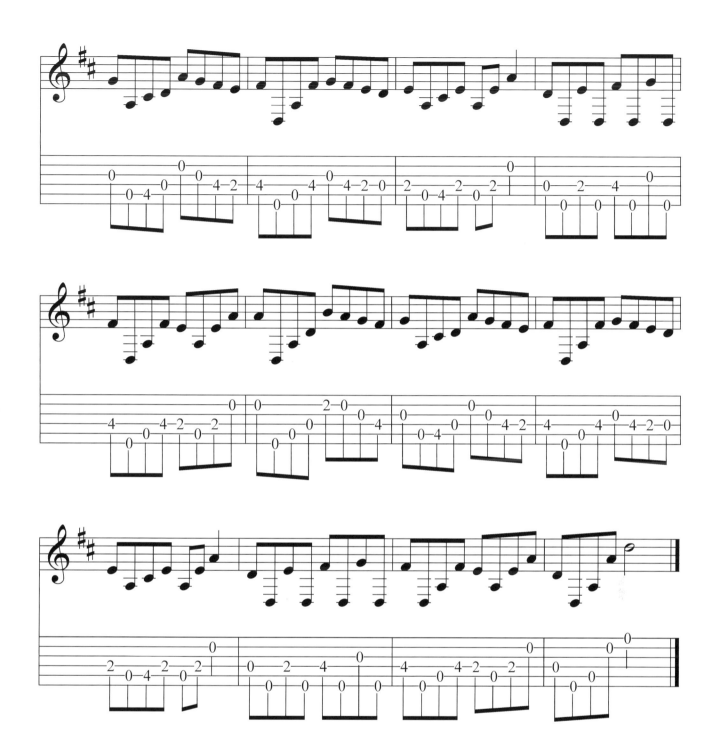

Away In A Manger

DADGAD

German Carol

Deck The Halls

DADGAD

English Traditional

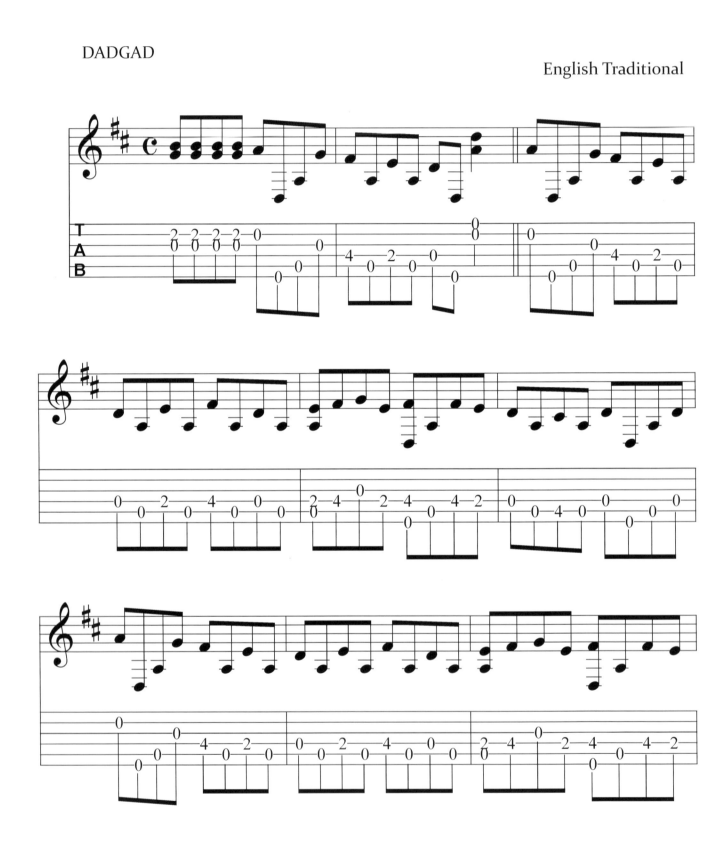

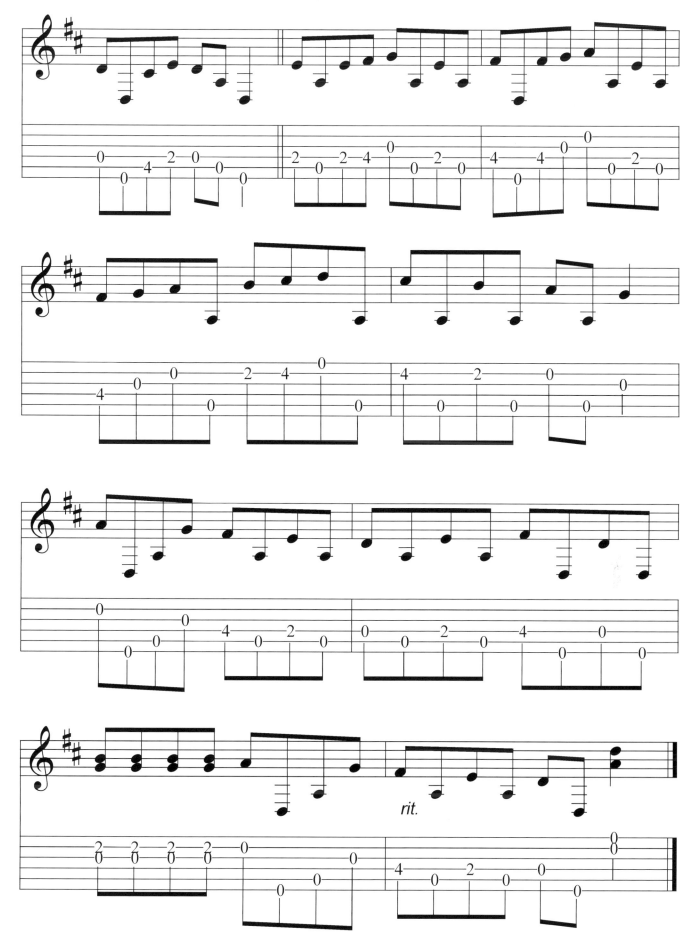

The First Noel

DADGAD

French Carol

let notes ring

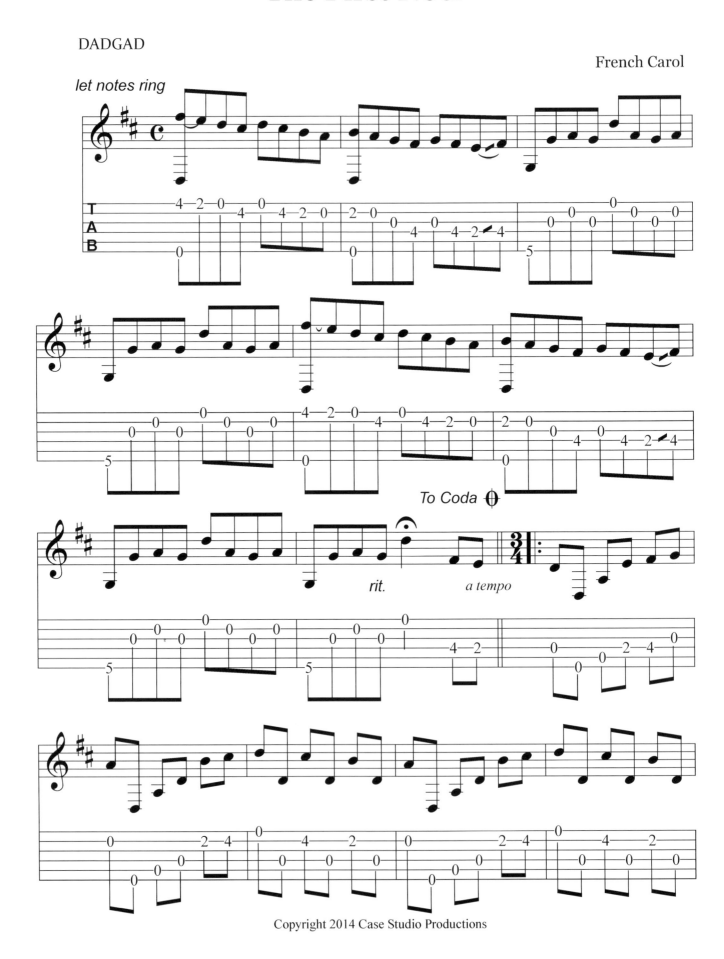

Joy To The World

DADGAD

Handel

D.S. al Coda

w/thumb

⊕ Coda

12th fret harmonics

15

Lullaby

DADGAD
Let Notes Ring Throughout

J. Case

rit.

Silent Night

DADGAD

Franz Gruber

Made in the USA
Coppell, TX
24 April 2023